It's Just A Thought...

By:

Vern H. Haynes, Jr.

It's Just A Thought…

By

Vern H. Haynes, Jr.

Published By:

ABM Publications
A division of Andrew Bills Ministries Inc.
PO Box 6811, Orange, CA 92863

www.abmpublications.com

ISBN: 978-1-931820-67-7

DEDICATION

To my wife Sandra, my five children,
and to Family Praise & Worship Church.

TABLE OF CONTENTS

Thought 1

ABUSE

A cheerful heart is good medicine, but a crushed spirit dries up the bones. **Proverb 17:22**

Abuse can take many forms.

Which one do you have?

Abuse is an emotion that is sometimes used to control others.

Abuse can sometimes be a wound carried from childhood to adulthood.

If you are being abused, maybe it's time to let God take over. What are you waiting for?

Is someone abusing you by brain washing you?

Some people seem to like being abused. It still doesn't make it right.

If you see no hope in life, then it is time to call Jesus.

Being verbally abused is abuse.

If abuse is costing you, maybe it's time to call on Jesus and get paid.

Being abused can cost you trust in people and in God.

Is your relationship out of control because of abuse?

A person who is not kind or cruel is not of Christ.

Why are you in an abusive relationship?

Abuse is not a gift of God

God does not abuse His children.

Were you ever an abusive person? If so, what are you doing about it?

Let your yes be yes when it comes to God and let your no be no to the world. **(read James 5:12)**

God can heal your broken heart and heal your land.

If you have been abused for a long time, maybe it's time to stand up and let God do the fighting.

The Fruit of the Spirit can heal you if you are willing.

Abuse can be a sin. Do not let it be a part of your life.

If you truly have Jesus in your life then abuse cannot be a part of your life.

Being verbally put down and belittled is abuse.

Thought 2

ACCOUNTABILITY

So then every one of us shall give account of himself to God. **Romans 14:12**

Accountability is a strange thing, because sometimes it can keep you from God.

There are many people who don't serve God because of accountability.

If God came this very minute, how would you account for your time on earth if He asked?

God wants us to be accountable to Him.

Being accountable to God keeps a true Christian close to God. What's keeping you close to God?

Accountability can be a part of obedience.

Pastors make the call for salvation but Satan uses accountability to keep people from God.

I wonder if God accepts our accountability.

Accountability can be the first step to salvation, but the second step is staying accountable.

Who or what are you accountable to?

Is being accountable to God one of your priorities?

Why is being accountable to God so important or is it?

Being accountable to God means that you will do whatever it takes to get to know Him and make Him every part of your life.

Accountability sometimes comes with fear, but the Bible says that God is not fear.

If people were not afraid of being accountable, maybe the church would be full.

Accountability with God can lead to new found freedom.

Accountability and responsibility can lead to faith.

Are you ready to give up your accountability with God?

Are you willing to give up your accountability with God?

Accountability can be everything with God.

Thought 3

ANXIETY

Cast all your anxiety on the Lord because He cares for you. **1 Peter 5:7**

When you have anxieties, do you wait on the Lord?

When you have anxieties, do you call on the Lord?

Do you call upon the Lord when you become stressed?

Stress is something that needs to be left to the Lord.

I am too blessed to be stressed is an old saying.

Maybe our anxieties are only a test.

Many times we place ourselves in a position to become stressed.

When you have anxieties, it is only for a season.

The best pill for an anxiety attack is the word of God.

The peace of God is a good remedy for anxieties.

Anxieties can lead to depression but try God first.

Ever wonder what causes anxieties? Maybe you don't have enough God.

Anxiety is nothing but a word, but God is life.

Who do you run to when you are stressed; is it God?

The word of God is life. So why are you stressed?

Do you believe that God cares for you? If so, why are you stressed?

God cares for you, so why stress?

If God cares for you there is no need to stress.

If God said to "cast all of your cares on Him," why are you holding back?

If God cares for you, why don't you?

Don't worry about what is not in your control.

I just wonder; if your anxiety is a lack of Faith in God?

Thought 4

BEING DEFINED

Then the LORD God formed a man from the dust of the ground and breathed into his nostrils the breath of life, and the man became a living being. **Genesis 2:7**

Your actions may be how people define you.

God wants you to know Him and to allow you to let your light shine.

Being defined by others could be a bad or good thing; it depends on your relationship with God.

It is better to be defined by God rather than by you.

Your make up is what defines who you are.

Your legacy is dependent on what defines you.

Many people define you by what they know about you.

Many people define you by what they don't know about you.

Your life will be defined before your life is over. Are you right with God?

Take the steps to leave the legacy you desire by

letting God be a part of who you are.

A life without God may not be the legacy you desire.

What you want in life may define your legacy.

A man who cannot control his desire must depend on his walk with God.

Controlling your desires can keep you out of trouble.

Some desires may not be the desires that one should act upon.

Are you the being that God created you to be?

Is it better to be defined by God or your fellowman?

What really defines you?

Being defined is not a desire that many of us think about until it is too late.

Being defined may not mean the same for all people. What does being defined mean to you?

Thought 5

BEING SAVED

For Christ also suffered once for sins, the righteous for the unrighteous, to bring you to God. He was put to death in the body but made alive in the Spirit. After being made alive, He went and made proclamation to the imprisoned spirits— to those who were disobedient long ago when God waited patiently in the days of Noah while the ark was being built. In it only a few people, eight in all, were saved through water, and this water symbolizes baptism that now saves you also—not the removal of dirt from the body but the pledge of a clear conscience toward God. It saves you by the resurrection of Jesus Christ, who has gone into heaven and is at God's right hand—with angels, authorities and powers in submission to him. **1 Peter 3:18-22**

Being saved is a blessing.

All Christians are saved but not always righteous.

Christ wants all of us to be saved. All Christians should seek out the lost and bring them closer to Christ.

Being saved is a commitment to Christ.

Being saved in Christ requires work.

Repenting is the first step to being saved.

Leaving the world and coming to Christ is like taking a bath.

Since God died on the cross for your sin, why not become saved in Christ?

You have to be right with God to maintain your standing with Him.

Have you placed your salvation in jeopardy by sin?

Give God what He desires…. all of you.

Being saved is something special in your life's journey.

Once you are saved, you should act like it.

When you are saved, you are on your way to heaven when Christ comes.

It will be up to you to stay obedient to His "Holy Word".

There will be many challenges that will confront you when you accept the Lord Jesus Christ as your Lord and Savior.

Have you ever said the Sinner's Prayer? Maybe it is time to say it and accept the Lord for who He is.

Thought 6

BELIEF

You say to God, 'My beliefs are flawless and I am pure in your sight.' **Job 11:4**

The belief you have in God will be a part of God determining your salvation.

When one accepts Christ, I just wonder if his/her belief changes.

Life makes many turns and many of those life turns are due to one's belief.

Belief can be the beginning of life with Christ.

The world is full of sin and chaos. I just wonder if belief is the root of all sin?

They say money is the root of evil, maybe belief is too.

Your belief may cause you to take the path for your life.

One's belief is a serious thing; it could be the beginning or the end of one's life.

Belief goes along with believing: what do you believe in?

We go through life and during that time we have seasons of good and bad times. Our beliefs drive us to make life long decision along the way. Are you willing to go the distance with your beliefs?

Is your belief in God stronger than your belief in the world?

How is your belief in God when trying times confront you?

Belief in your struggles can lead you to Christ.

Your belief in Christ can help you to sustain the struggles of life.

Belief in God can be a life saver.

Belief in your struggles can lead you to Christ.

Your belief in Christ can help you to sustain the struggles of life.

Your belief may define who you are.

Is your belief flawless in God?

Will your belief in God allow you to enter heaven?

Thought 7

CHANGE

Therefore, I urge you, brothers and sisters, in view of God's mercy, to offer your bodies as a living sacrifice, holy and pleasing to God—this is your true and proper worship. Do not conform to the pattern of this world, but be transformed by the renewing of your mind. Then you will be able to test and approve what God's will is—his good, pleasing and perfect will. **Romans 12:1-2**

It's never too late in God's eyes to change.

Once you accept the Lord as your Savior, don't look back!

Many of us have given up and allowed the world to rule our lives instead of God.

Remember, your body belongs to Christ.

When you accept Christ, your thinking starts to change.

When you accept Christ, your life starts to change.

Change is good when God is in it.

Many of us fight change when God calls us to Him.

It is hard to let go of the world and seek Christ instead, but it is worth it.

God will give us new habits.

When you accept Christ and change for Him, Satan will work hard to get you back.

If you feel the change of God coming over you, why fight it?

Changing for God is a good thing.

When a man of God comes out of the world, not only does it please God, but it is pleasing to the man's wife too.

When a woman of God comes out of the world, not only does it please God, but it is pleasing to the woman's husband too.

God can change a bad marriage into a great marriage.

Are you willing to change for Christ

Do you trust God with your life?   If so, then change for Him.

Stepping out in faith is a good change.

Following God's holy word is a change from the world.

God can change you for the best if you will let Him.

We know that in all things God works for the good for those who love Him.

God will never give you more than you can handle.

"If God brings you to it, He will bring you through it."

You are too blessed to be stressed. Let go and let God!

Remember that God is God and you should have no other before him.

Change is a word that many people fear.

Change is not easy. Change is not always good.

When you change so does the world around you.

Take the challenge and change for God.

God can change you if you let Him.

God never changes, He is always the same.

God is the same now as He was before you were born.

Don't change for others but change for God.

When seeking Christ it is hard to let go of the world.

Thought 8

CHRISTMAS

And the angel said to them, "Fear not, for behold, I bring you good news of great joy that will be for all the people." **Luke 2:10**

Is Christmas a time for gifts or love?

Christmas is a time of joy, love and peace. Is it for you?

Christmas is a time to remember Christ.

Christ died on the cross and Christmas is the time to remember Him.

Many people go into debt during Christmas, but that was not the plan.

Christians need to remember the real meaning of Christmas. Do you know the real meaning of Christmas?

Christians need to remember that a child was born this day and He was called Jesus.

Christmas day should be the one day to bring joy to the World. How do you feel about Christmas?

Where does Santa Claus fit in your belief of Christmas, or does he?

Christmas is a time to bring your loved one's closer together, not to push them further away from each other!

Christians should treat each day as if it were Christmas.

Christmas is the one day in the year when the world seems to come closer together.

Many people light up their homes on Christmas. Have you tried to light up your heart?

Christ died for the people of this world. Do you deserve it?

Christmas should be about family because Christ gave up His life for His bride.

Christmas should be about family. Isn't the body of Christ family?

Do you honor Christmas as Christ honors you?

Do you respect Christ for what He did for mankind?

Christ died to give us a second chance. Are you making the best of life?

Christmas is a time of giving joy. Are you giving joy to others?

What is Christmas without Christ?

Christmas is a time for all people but not all people know the real meaning of the season.

People, as well as God's people, have forgotten the "Good News" that was received that day.

Christmas should be a time of joy, but for many it is a time of sadness.

Not all people receive the "Good News", but there are some who are not sure how to receive it.

Are you sharing the "Good News" about Christmas?

What is the "Good News"?

Jesus Christ was born on that day for a reason.

Jesus is the reason for the season.

The "Good News" is that Christ was born to save a person like you.

Are you worthy to receive the "Good News"?

There is no reason to fear because Christ was born to bring joy to the world.

Fear brings despair but Christ is of peace, joy and love.

Children love Christmas; teach them to love Jesus the same way.

Christmas is not a time to go into debt.

Have you thought about going through the Christmas season debt free?

Don't get caught up in spending money you don't have during Christmas.

Don't let people mislead you during the Christmas season.

Do you honor God on Christmas day?

Do you honor or respect the reason for the season?

Shouldn't we honor Christ on Christmas and along with our parents and loved ones?

Why is Christmas special to you, or is it?

Churches come together during Christmas but why wait until then?

Christmas is a time to bring joy to the world, but we should bring joy to the world every day.

Christmas is a time to bring joy to the world, but it should bring joy to the world every day.

Thought 9

CHURCH

Keep watch over yourselves and all the flock of which the Holy Spirit has made you overseers. Be shepherds of the church of God, which he bought with his own blood. **Acts 20:28**

There are those who say they love the Lord, but refuse to worship with His church.

Many say that they know the Lord but refuse to be accountable to God's church.

Many love God at home through their television.

There are those who love the Lord but refuse to be accountable to the shepherds that God has placed to watch over their church.

Those who refuse to join a church may be in fear that they will be exposed of their lack of knowledge about God.

Are you doing everything possible for Christ? If so, then support your church in tithes and offering.

Church is a place of Worship and to spend time with the Lord. What is keeping you from joining a church?

The Church is like a meeting place to date Christ and let Him know that you love Him.

God calls the church His bride. If you know this, then what is keeping you from saying "I Do"?

God wants you to be a part of a church to have someone over you to teach you.

Being involved in a church can bring joy to your heart.

Being a part of a church is part of God's plan to ensure that the shepherd can watch over you.

Church is a vital part of getting to know who Christ is.

Do you have a church home? If not, what are you waiting for? Church can be an uncomfortable place when you are fighting God.

Church is a place of healing. If you don't have a family, try the family of God.

The church is a place of comfort and peace.

The people make up God's church.

Thought 10

CHURCH MEMBERSHIP

They were continually devoting themselves to the apostles' teaching and to fellowship, to the breaking of bread and to prayer. **Acts 2:42**

Are you willing to be devoted in having a pastor over you who will assist you in your walk with the Lord?

Maybe it is time to join a church family; to break bread and pray.

Are you involved in a church that is Bible based?

Are you a church member who is committed to attend, love, serve, and submit to your church?

What is keeping you from joining a church?

Are you doing the right thing by not being a member of a church?

Are you attending church and becoming involved? Do you know if you're in good standing with your church?

Do you know how to be in good standing with a church?

Being a member of a church is being right with God.

How valuable are you as a member of your church?

Do you have any value in your church?

Do you love the Lord enough to be committed to a church?

Along with membership to a church comes responsibility and accountability.

Responsibility and accountability many times keep one from being committed to a church.

When you become a member of a church, it shows your commitment to God.

Don't say yes to the Lord until you're ready to go all the way.

Being a member of a church will provide you with guidance in your walk with the Lord.

When was the last time you broke bread with your church family?

Are you truly a family member in God's kingdom?

Thought 11

COMMUNICATION

Do not let any unwholesome talk come out of your mouths, but only what is helpful for building others up according to their needs, that it may benefit those who listen. **Ephesians 4:29**

Communication is vital to having a peaceful life.

When an individual learns to share his or her inner thoughts with those in his/her life, the door of the world opens.

A man and woman who are married must learn to communicate with each other. Why? Because that is what God would want them to do.

The ability to communicate is the key of sharing one's inner self.

When was the last time you prayed?

When you communicate with Christ, make sure you can listen too.

True communication can be the rope that ties two people together; it's called love.

Communication can open the doors of the world.

Is your inability to communicate keeping you from moving forward in your life?

Is pride keeping you from communicating with others and God?

When God calls you, do you respond?

Being able to communicate is like learning how to walk.

God will take the inadequate and give them the gift to communicate effectively.

Communication can be power if used correctly, but on the other hand, it could be a person's down-fall.

Men at all times should communicate with their wives.

Women at all times should communicate with their husbands.

Many of you use God's name in vain. Is that the way God wants you to communicate?

Are you keeping the doors of communication open with the Lord?

Many people slam the door of communication on the Lord when the struggles of world are upon them.

Thought 12

CONTROLLING SPIRIT

"For the LORD God is a sun and shield: the LORD will give grace and glory: no good thing will He withhold from them that walk uprightly." **Psalm 84:11**

Are you in control of your life?

Having the spirit of God in your life will allow you to be blessed.

Are you aware of what is controlling your life?

Are you allowing others to control you?

Your walk with God is vital to your salvation and receiving eternal life.

Anger is a spirit that can do harm to you and others.

A controlling spirit can ruin a friendship.

Do you know if a controlling spirit is ruining your life?

If you're out of control, maybe it's time to take a look in the mirror.

Are you walking in the light of God?

A controlling spirit can ruin a marriage.

Do not let the spirit of anger control you.

Do not let the spirit of laziness control your life.

Do not become involved in the spirit of witchcraft.

A controlling spirit can ruin a relationship.

Getting others to do what you want without their understanding, is a controlling spirit.

Manipulating people and circumstances for personal advantage is not of God.

Repentance to God is a lifetime commitment.

God is a forgiving God; do not let unforgiveness pull you down.

Let go of self and let God be in control.

Who is in control of your life, God or the world?

Stay true to God who rules over you.

Thought 13

CREATOR

Do you not know? Have you not heard? The
LORD is the everlasting God, the Creator of the
ends of the earth. He will not grow tired or weary,
and his understanding no one can fathom.
Isaiah 40: 27-29

At the end of the day all you have is the One who
created it.

Once you have heard who He is, now the seed has
been planted who He is.

If God created heaven and earth, why not give God
the respect for creating you?

If you are tired and weary, are you living in this
world without the Lord?

We are quick to give others credit, why not give
the Creator His credit.

We are slow to turn to our Creator in our time of
need, but quick to turn to man.

The Creator has the power, not man.

The Creator helps us in our journey of life.

Who do you turn to, the world or the Creator?

How do you define who the creator is?

There is only one creator and that is God.

Does man understand us in our time of need like God?

At what point do we stop calling on man and let God have his way with us.

If God created man and woman to live in peace, what is the problem?

The Creator is not given enough credit by man.

Our blessings come from our Creator.

Who is your Creator?

If God is your creator, why do you not pray to Him?

Praying to your Creator is one way to hopefully find out what He wants of you.

The Creator should be number one in your life.

Thought 14

DELILAH

After putting him to sleep on her lap, she called for someone to shave off the seven braids of his hair, and so began to subdue him. And his strength left him. **Judges 16:19**

Samson was overcome by Delilah, so what makes you so special?

Everyone has a Delilah haunting them.

Who or what is your Delilah?

Always be on the lookout for Delilah.

Delilah is someone or something that is evil.

Delilah wants to separate you from God.

The only way to fight Delilah is to keep your covenant with God.

Delilah comes in all forms and shapes.

Remember, that all that glitters is not gold.

The thief comes in the night, but Delilah comes in the day and night.

Delilah can disrupt your peace.

Always be on the look-out for Delilah.

Our walk with God should prepare us for the Delilahs of the world.

The world is full of Delilahs.

The Delilahs of the world can take you to a place that God doesn't want you to be; it's called Hell.

The Delilahs of this world want to destroy you.

Delilah can be conquered by God's Holy word.

Meditate on Christ and stay strong to fight Delilah another day.

Delilahs can be your worst enemy.

Remember, that all that glitters is not God.

Thought 15

DESIRE

Take delight in the LORD, and he will give you the desires of your heart. **Psalm 37:4**

Have you ever had a desire for something but could never reach it?

Have you ever had a desire that was close enough to reach, but someone told you that you were not worthy?

Have you ever wanted something, but did not know how to get it?

Have you had a desire for love and felt that you would never find that type of love again?

A desire is something hard to acquire.

How does it feel to want but no one wants to help you fulfill that desire?

How great is your desire for life? Is your desire to know God as strong as your desire to live life?

A desire is something from within that wants to express itself on the outside.

Is your desire yours or someone else's?

What is your desire?

Do you have a desire to live life as God desires for you?

A desire to belong to a certain group of people may not be a good thing.

Your desire to achieve something in life may destroy who you are.

Have the desire to follow your own heart and not someone else's.

Having a desire for something is not always a good thing.

Having the right Godly desire can take you where you need to be in life.

Is your desire a light for others to see?

Desire is just a word, or is it? What does desire mean to you?

What is your desire when it comes to the Lord?

Thought 16

DREAMS

The angel of God said to me in the dream, "Jacob". I answered, "Here I am." **Genesis 31:11**

Having a dream that all of God's people will come together as one is a great thing to dream!

As a Christian it is good to dream of world peace.

As you dream, remember where your dreams come from.

It's good to dream when God is part of the dream or the end of the dream.

As a Christian we should dream of peace among all men.

Having a dream of bringing Christians together as one is a lifetime dream.

When you dream, what do you dream?

Dreams should be special.

Christ can talk to you in your dreams.

Sometimes you have no choice but to listen when Christ talks to you in your dreams.

Dreams can be special when they turn out to be positive.

Are your dreams pure in heart?

Some people are afraid to dream; maybe they need to have Christ in them.

Dreams can sometimes allow you to reach your goals.

Are your goals a part of your dreams?

Dreams give you a focus of where you want to go.

Dreams give you a focus as to what you want to become.

Never let anyone steal your dreams.

Dreams may not be for everyone.

Do you dream? If so, do you hear God?

Is a dream hard to obtain in life?

Good dreams can be healthy.

Thought 17

FEAR

He will cover you with his feathers, and under his wings you will find refuge; his faithfulness will be your shield and rampart.[5] You will not fear the terror of night, nor the arrow that flies by day,[6] nor the pestilence that stalks in the darkness, nor the plague that destroys at midday.[7] A thousand may fall at your side, ten thousand at your right hand, but it will not come near you. **Psalm 91:4-7**

If you know God you should have no fear.

If you have God in you, there's no need to fear life.

Trusting God will allow God to protect you.

Fear is of the world and not of God.

If God is protecting you, why should you fear the things of the world?

Fear can keep you from moving forward.

Fear can lead you to failure and unhappiness.

Fear can keep you at a standstill.

Where is your fear coming from?

Why do you allow fear to play such a great part in your life?

What is greater, fear or the love of God?

Is fear controlling your life?

Fear is not the Spirit of God.

Fear is like a shadow that follows you around.

Some people wake up looking at fear.

Don't let fear control your life; let God be in control.

Maybe it is time to face your fears and allow God to help you conquer them.

If you do not know how to fight your fear, ask God.

Fear can keep you faithless.

Fear is one of the biggest fights in your life.

Stand with God and He will help you fight your fears.

Thought 18

FRIENDS

Greater love has no one than this; that someone lay down his life for his friends. **John 15:13**

Friends are people that you can depend on.

A friend is someone you do not have to look for when you're in need.

A friend will never turn his/her back on you.

Someone who knows your inner feelings is a friend.

When good times come into your life, it is nice to have a friend to share those moments.

A godly friend can bring true love to your heart.

How great is your friendship with Christ? Did you know that Jesus can be a friend?

What a friend you can have in Jesus, if you want it.

It would be awful to lose Jesus as a friend.

Your wife or husband on earth should be your best friend.

Would your husband or wife lay down his/her life

for you? Jesus did.

A friend is someone that you do not have to look very far for.

A friend is someone you can trust.

Does your closest friend love God?

What a friend you have in Jesus. All you have to do is ask.

A good friend is hard to find but a godly friend is even harder.

Always treat your friends right.

A true friend has an honest, sincere quality about himself or herself.

Having a true friend is special.

Thank Jesus for giving you a friend on this earth.

Are you a friend to someone like Jesus is to you?

Thought 19

FRIENDSHIP

You adulterous people, don't you know that friendship with the world means enmity against God? Therefore, anyone who chooses to be a friend of the world becomes an enemy of God. **James 4:4**

How do you define friendship?

Friendship is something that is hard to find.

When you find a friend, it can be something hard to keep.

Friendship is like love. Do you ever find it?

When you're married, you should have a strong friendship with your spouse.

What is friendship? Can a man and woman have a friendship and be nothing else?

Why does the world frown upon a single man having a friendship with a married woman?

Is it really an impossibility?

Why does the world frown upon a single woman having a friendship with a married man? Is it really impossibility?

Friendship is something that is special to the heart and soul.

A true friend is like a diamond that you want to keep for a life time.

True friendship is desired by everyone.

Not everyone finds friendship.

Friendship comes once in a lifetime.

Friendship is something that can endure struggles in life.

You do not have to look for friends during times of struggles and conflict because they are always there for you.

Friendship-what does it mean to you?

Do you have a friendship in your life?

Friendships are special and hard to fine.

Is there a friendship between you and your spouse?

Thought 20

GIVING

Be careful not to practice your righteousness in front of others to be seen by them. If you do, you will have no reward from your Father in heaven. "So when you give to the needy, do not announce it with trumpets, as the hypocrites do in the synagogues and on the streets, to be honored by others. Truly I tell you, they have received their reward in full. But when you give to the needy, do not let your left hand know what your right hand is doing, so that your giving may be in secret. Then your Father, who sees what is done in secret, will reward you.   **Matthew 6:1-4**

When you give, it should be out of the goodness of your heart.

Giving to Christ is nothing to boast about.

Giving is not about you.

If you are looking for others to recognize you regarding your giving to the Lord, you are approaching God the wrong way.

God is a giving God.

We all need to learn to give as God wants us to.

Tithing is a form of giving but it needs to be from a willing heart.

Do you tithe with a willing heart or do you give because the Bible says so?

Giving to God is hard for most people who love the Lord.

Those that make a lot of money find it hard to tithe.

If you give to the needy, God will bless you.

Don't ever give to God looking for a blessing.

Blessings will come when you give with a pure heart.

No man can beat God at giving.

Let the love for God be the force behind your giving.

Tithing is being obedient to God.

When was the last time you gave to Christ in the form of service?

Have you given God the best gift you possess? That would be yourself.

Thought 21

HOLIDAYS

Let no man therefore judge you in meat, or in drink, or in respect of an Holyday, or of the new moon, or of the Sabbath days. **Colossians 2:16**

New Year's Day comes once a year, but God is around all year long.

When we make our resolutions on New Year's, many times God is not part of the resolutions. If we were to make God our main resolution maybe the year would be fulfilling.

Valentine's Day is known for cupid, roses, candy and love. What a wonderful day to have. The sad thing about Valentine's Day is that some of us only give and receive roses, candy and love on this one day. God wants every day to be a happy one. Remember, every day is God's day. If this is true, we should have roses, candy and love every day of the year.

Valentine's Day is a time that many couples get married. It is a day that the most marriages occur during a year. If it is a day for marriage, how does Christ fit in?

Most of the world gets lost in the Easter bunny during Easter. We need to remember that Easter is the resurrection of Jesus Christ.

Easter is a time to remember that Christ died for our sins. That is why we call it Resurrection Sunday. If we are teaching our kids and others about the Easter bunny, then what happens to Christ on this day?

Christ died to save the lost. You were lost one day but you found your way to Christ. What is your next step and will you continue to take it?

Christ rose from the dead and His Holy word says he will return. Will you be ready?

Are you really thankful for what God has done for you?

Thanksgiving is a day to give thanks to the Lord. When was the last time you gave thanks to the Lord?

Life is full of wonders but it lasts for just a moment. Be grateful for the little things, and God will bless you with the abundance of life.

Do people look at Christmas as a time of receiving gifts or a time to show your gift of God?

Is God part of the holiday spirit during Thanksgiving and Christmas?

When was the last time you thanked God during the Holidays?

Why is it so hard to put Christ first during the holidays?

Thought 22

HOPE

Through whom we have gained access by faith into this grace in which we now stand. And we boast in the hope of the glory of God. Not only so, but we also glory in our sufferings, because we know that suffering produces perseverance; perseverance, character; and character, hope. And hope does not put us to shame, because God's love has been poured out into our hearts through the Holy Spirit, who has been given to us. **Romans 5:2-5**

Some people have no hope at all.

Trusting God can make hope a reality.

Hope is the end results of Faith.

Hope can provide a reason to live.

God is hope.

Without God in our lives there is no real hope.

How can one have hope and not have God in their lives?

What are you hoping for?

With God all things are possible.

Hope can be the end result of happiness.

We hope for many things in life.

Hope is not just a word, it can bring life to many people.

Sometimes hope is all people have.

Never give up hoping.

Many times hope is combined with faith in God.

Hope can lead to faith.

When times get hard, never lose hope in God.

Hope and Faith in God can bring you to the good times.

When hope is fulfilled it can bring joy to your heart.

Hope may be everything in your journey in life.

Thought 23

HUSBANDS

Husbands, love your wives, as Christ loved the church and gave himself up for her. **Ephesians 5:25**

The Bible says to love your wives and to not be harsh with them.

Do you love your wife?

Are your actions a reflection of Christ?

If so, then there is no reason for your wife to doubt you.

Are you being the godly man that God wants you to be?

Is your love for Christ reflected in the way you treat your wife?

Not every man can be a good husband.

Every man should know and love Jesus before becoming a husband.

If you treat Jesus right, you will treat your wife right.

Never expect your wife to submit to you until you learn to submit to Christ.

How can a husband be committed in a marriage when he is not committed to Christ?

A real husband has no problem kneeling and praying to God.

A godly husband will be a godly example.

A husband who is the head of his household should be following God's Holy Word.

Have you ever thought about what kind of husband you are?

Are you a godly husband if not, why?

A husband's body belongs to his wife.

Do you treat your wife according to man or God?

Have you ever thought about why your wife doesn't respect you?

If you respect God, your wife will respect you.

Show love for your wife the way Christ shows love for the church.

Is your wife truly your treasure?

Thought 24

LIVING WATERS

He that believeth on me, as the scripture hath said, out of his belly shall flow rivers of living waters. **John 7:38**

God created water and everything in it.

Have you chosen to accept Jesus Christ as your Lord and Savior?

Did you know that when you accepted Jesus Christ as your Lord and Savior you were sealed with the Holy Spirit?

There is a mystery about the substance of water.

There is no life without water. Remember God created it.

God will allow our spirit man to draw Holy water from His living well.

When Jesus was at the well, He asked the woman, "Will you give me a drink?"

God will give you living water if you ask Him. Everyone who drinks God's living water will not thirst again.

God is the fountain of life; will you drink from His

fountain?

Only Christ can give water that will satisfy the desire of the soul.

Is the water that is in you stagnate or purified?

When you do not allow the Holy Spirit to operate in you, you are like a dry river bed.

What kind of water are you drinking?

Drinking the wrong water is not good for you.

The living water of Christ will lead to eternal life.

Why take a sip of the living water when you can take a gulp?

Try a gulp of the living water; you just might like it.

There is no other water like the living water of Jesus Christ.

Remember, Christ was baptized in water.

The world in Noah's time was cleansed by water.

The world is dependent on water, so why can't you be dependent on Christ?

Thought 25

LOVE

For God so loved the world, that He gave His only begotten Son, that whosoever believeth in Him should not perish, but have everlasting life. John 3:16

Some say that love makes the world go around, God created the world.

If you love the Lord, does your life reflect Him?

God gave up His Son for us. What have you given to God lately?

In order for a married man and a woman to truly love one another, they first need to love God.

Love can conquer hate but many of us have not mastered the gift of love.

Many times when married couples are not getting along, one may ask the question, "how are you getting along with God?"

When one truly finds the meaning of love, it can sometimes hurt.

You say you love God, but your actions say otherwise. Why don't you believe in Him?

If a man says he doesn't love himself, how can he love you?

Many times when couples get married, they forget to have God in the mix.

Love is said to be a word that cannot be defined or expressed in words. If this is true, how does God express His love for us?

If God said that everlasting life is based on love, would you believe it?

When you believe that your marriage is finished, maybe it is time to give God a chance.

If you say you love God, maybe it is time to act like it.

Did God give His life for you for nothing?

Are you willing to perish because you do not believe in God?

Love can lead to everlasting life.

How much love do you have for Christ?

Love lifted Christ on the cross.

Thought 26

LOYALTY

Those who prove to be disloyal are those who prove they do not belong to Him. **1 John 3:24**.

Loyalty can be everything in one's life.

Loyalty is something that can be hard to find.

A person who is loyal is not necessarily a good person.

God wants your loyalty.

Being loyal to God is a giant step toward your salvation.

Are you loyal to God?

Where does your loyalty lie, in man or God?

What does it take for you to be loyal to God?

Not everyone has the gift of being loyal to someone, especially to God.

Some people's loyalty lies in the game of golf and not in God.

Some people's loyalty lays in sports on television

on Sunday and not God.

Many people's loyalty is tested on Sundays.

What is loyalty without love?

Loyalty is something that comes from within and is sometimes unexplainable.

Some would say trust and loyalty work hand in hand.

Some say loyalty will develop with love.

There are many people who are loyal to the world and not to God.

Are you loyal to God's kingdom? It's called a church.

With loyalty comes power.

Loyalty allows a person a feeling of belonging to someone or something.

God is promising His loyalty and commitment to us.

Christ calls us to be steadfast and loyal.

Christ expects loyalty. Do you expect God's loyalty?

A true believer's loyalty is shown in his/her commitment to Jesus and His gospel.

Thought 27

LUST

So I say, walk by the Spirit, and you will not gratify the desires of the flesh. For the flesh desires what is contrary to the Spirit, and the Spirit what is contrary to the flesh. They are in conflict with each other, so that you are not to do whatever you want. **Galatians 5:16-17**

Lust is something that you desire that is not good for you.

Lust could be the means to an end.

Is your lust in life with God?

Is your Spirit in control of your lust?

How is your walk in life?

The spirit of lust can lead to your destruction.

Is what you desire of lust?

Lust can be worst then the loss of money.

Maybe you need to put your lust in check.

The doors to lust are your eyes.

Can lust ever lead to happiness?

Is the spirit of lust leading you or the spirit of God?

What is the strongest spirit in you, the spirit of lust or the spirit of God?

Lust can trap your heart.

The spirit of lust can make you take the wrong turn in your journey of life.

Lust is a good thing if it is your wife or husband.

When lust shows up at your door, maybe you should leave the door close.

Lust could be a good reason to turn around and run.

Lust can destroy your life.

If you think you can handle the spirit of lust on your own, think again.

Guard your heart against the spirit of lust.

Thought 28

MARRIAGE

Husbands, love your wives, even as Christ also loved the church, and gave Himself for it. **Ephesians 5:25**

How many men love their wives, as Christ loves the church? Most men don't love the church.

Marriage is like a car that needs to be regularly tuned-up.

Marriage can be hard at times but if God is in the center of your marriage, you can get through it.

Before getting married, you need to get your relationship with Christ right first.

Some people get married with their eyes closed. This is the time you need to open your heart to Christ and ask for his guidance.

The Bible says that if man does not love himself then he can't love his wife.

How can you say you love God, but your actions reflect differently? In a marriage sanctioned by God, you must have the love of God.

Marriage sanctioned by God is a gift from God.

Seeking God in your life will help you to do the right thing when you are ready to get married.

What is keeping you in your marriage?

If marriage is a covenant between a man and woman, what is the covenant between man and God?

Do you have a covenant with God?

If your marriage is not right, maybe it is time to put Christ in the center of you marriage.

If you are not right with God, maybe you are not ready to get married.

Many marriages come and go, but if God is in your marriage you will stay.

Marriage is like a close relationship with God, after all God calls his people His bride.

Before you say "I do" to God, think about it.

If your marriage is in shambles, most likely so is your relationship with Christ.

Keeping a relationship with Christ is not easy.

Marriage can be wonderful if you keep Christ in it.

Thought 29

MEDITATION

I can do all things through him who gives me strength. **Philippians 4:13**

The more time we spend meditating on God's word, the more we will reap the benefits from the His "Holy Word".

Meditation means to reflect on or ponder on His word.

The more time we spend thinking about the word, the more power and ability we will have.

The more knowledge we have about God, the more revelation we will receive from the Word.

Meditation is a time to reflect. The problem is that many of us do not slow down to meditate with God.

When was the last time you were in your prayer closet? If it has been a while, you're missing out on personal time with God.

When you stop from your busy schedule to meditate on God, you will learn something about yourself.

Meditation on God is healthy.

When you stop and pray, I believe that you are meditating with the Lord.

If you are waiting for the Lord, it would be a good time to mediate.

How many times have you tried to do things that needed to be left up to God?

Some say that mediation is good for the soul, but God is better.

Meditating on God is for those who need it.

Meditating on God helps the heart to heal.

The more you meditate with God, the more your life will improve.

Do you ever use a prayer closet to meditate?

Do you meditate on Christ?

Meditation with God can lead to a healthy life.

How often do you meditate on God?

Meditating on God can take the weight of the world off of your heart.

Some say that meditating can take the weight off of your shoulders.

Thought 30

ONE GOD

For there is one God and one mediator between God and mankind, the man Christ Jesus. **1 Timothy 2:5**

Remember there is only one God.

Many people put drugs, sports, television and lust before God. What's your excuse?

Our God is alive. Is yours?

Who or what is your God?

Many people cannot serve God because of excuses.

God is waiting for you. What is holding you back?

Remember that God has given you all that you have.

Our life depends on the one and only God; His name is Jesus.

Jesus is the reason for the season.

If you know Jesus, then you know God.

God has said, "You will have no other God before me."

Have you placed an idol or anything before God?

Excuses can become a barrier for some.

Serving God is a commitment to Him.

Are you a witness for Jesus Christ?

God is the Alpha and the Omega.

God was there in the beginning when no one else was present.

When you have God, nothing else matters.

Our lives should start with Christ and end with Christ.

In the beginning was the Word, and the Word was with God, and the Word was God. **John 1:1**

Thought 31

PASTOR

Here is a trustworthy saying: Whoever aspires to be an overseer desires a noble task. Now the overseer is to be above reproach, faithful to his wife, temperate, self-controlled, respectable, hospitable, able to teach, not given to drunkenness, not violent but gentle, not quarrelsome, not a lover of money. He must manage his own family well and see that his children obey him, and he must do so in a manner worthy of full respect. (If anyone does not know how to manage his own family, how can he take care of God's church?) He must not be a recent convert, or he may become conceited and fall under the same judgment as the devil. He must also have a good reputation with outsiders, so that he will not fall into disgrace and into the devil's trap. **1 Timothy 3:1-7**

There is a high expectation that is placed on a Pastor but none higher than what God expects.

Are you a Pastor? If so, how trustworthy are you?

Are you, as a Pastor, able to meet the expectations of **1 Timothy 3: 1-7?**

Is your house in good order? Is your home a godly home for others to see?

As a Pastor you are required to walk the walk and talk the talk; are you?

Being an overseer of Gods' people can become tiresome but Christ will renew you.

Pastor's children can be a thorn in their life if they let them.

A Pastor should not only oversee his flock, but his home as well.

A Pastor must manage his own integrity. A Pastor's work is never done.

Being a Pastor can be a lonely ministry. Sometimes Pastors feel that everyone is against them.

A Pastor needs to learn to take a time-out (vacation) to recharge himself/herself.

Having time to reflect is a must for a Pastor. A Pastor should always spend time meditating and praying with God.

Sometimes finding good help is hard to find.

As a Pastor, who do you depend on other than God?

A Pastor needs someone other than God to talk to.

How many times when the Pastor asks you to help in the church, you say, "I have to pray on it." Hum.

Thought 32

PATIENCE

Be patient, then, brothers and sisters, until the Lord's coming. See how the farmer waits for the land to yield its valuable crop, patiently waiting for the autumn and spring rains. **James 5:7**

What type of patience do you possess?

Where does your patience come from, the world or God?

Maybe the struggles you're going through are just the testing of your patience.

Patience is hard to fine and keep when you're facing trials and struggles.

Can one truly be patient when facing struggles? Ask God.

In obtaining our salvation we must have patience.

Living in a world of people, patience is a requirement.

What is your patience level?

If you do not possess any patience, talk to God.

Patience is a gift from God and it is something hard to keep.

Some never find patience.

God can give you patience when you are ready to give up the world.

Patience and love go together, especially in a marriage sanctioned by God.

If there is no patience in a marriage, the marriage will not survive.

Getting to know God requires some patience.

Are you waiting for the Lord?

Not everyone has the gift of patience, do you?

Patience can sometimes be the testing of your faith.

Are you pursuing patience or is it pursuing you?

Patience-how do you define it?

Thought 33

PEACE

A time to love and a time to hate; a time for war and a time for peace. **Ecclesiastes 3:8**

Everyone wants peace. Do you?

Peace is hard to come by for many of us.

Some people do not know what peace is.

How do you define peace?

The world does not know how to obtain world peace.

Will mankind ever see world peace?

What will give you peace?

Is your life full of peace?

Do not let anger, hate, abuse and pride keep you from having peace.

The love of God can bring you peace.

You have a better chance of obtaining peace with Christ than without Him.

Peace can give you a better life; try God.

If you did not know that God could help you get peace, you do now.

Wouldn't it be wonderful to have everlasting peace?

Peace comes from within; is Christ in you?

Man will never have peace when he is of the world.

Man must come to Christ if we are to ever have world peace.

If you do not have peace, maybe it's time to try Jesus.

Peace should be the goal of all mankind.

When God grants your salvation and you receive eternal life, you will have peace.

Did you know that true peace will be in heaven with our Lord and Savior?

When you leave this earth, my prayer for you will be to rest in His peace.

Thought 34

PERSPECTIVE

As the heavens are higher than the earth, so are my ways higher than your ways and my thoughts than your thoughts. **Isaiah 55:9**

Do you have the perspective to persevere even when the world is against you?

Your perspective could be your downfall.

Perspective could be your guiding light in your journey through life.

Do you know what your perspective is on life?

How has your perspective been affecting your life?

What is your perspective based on?

Your perspective can affect your perseverance in life.

Are your goals in life tied to your perspective on life?

One's perspectives on Christ are based on one's life experiences or are they?

Is your perspective on life in line with God's?

Can your perspective in life be defined?

Do you have the desire to have your perspective in line with God?

Is your perspective taking you in the right direction?

Having the right perspective on Christ is vital.

One's perspective can take you to a high place with Christ if you allow Him to use you.

One's perspective can remove and keep out the junk in one's life.

Perspective must be developed early in one's life.

Can one truly live without a positive perspective on Christ?

What perspective do you have on being involved in God's Kingdom (church)?

One's perspective will have an impact on his/hers outlook on life.

Thought 35

POWER

But if it is by the finger of God that I cast out demons, then the kingdom of God has come upon you. **Luke 11:20**

God can give us the gift to cast out demons in our lives, but many times we try to handle our demons by ourselves.

Power is something people strive for, but in the end the power overtakes them.

A nation with too much power may not survive.

Power can lift a man up, but power can also tear a man down.

Many say money is power. If that's the case, where does God fit in?

The power of God can give you focus in life but power alone can destroy your life.

Not every man can handle power. Some people wait for power for a lifetime. Some get it quicker.

God has the power to create change.

What kind of power do you have?

The power that you have is the power that God has given you.

If knowledge is power, then why do so many people misuse it?

Are you using the power that God has given you?

Have you ever thought that the power that God has given you is called a gift?

Knowing God is power in itself.

Power is something that people search for a lifetime and never find it.

Man defines knowledge as power, but God is power.

Sometimes power can affect members of a church.

If not used properly, power can get in the way of your relationship with Christ.

Where does your power come from?

What kind of power do you have?

Thought 36

PRIORITY

For where your treasure is, there will your heart be also. **Luke 12:34**

Is God your priority?

What is the priority in your life's journey?

Priority with God could lead to eternal life.

Do you whine when it comes to having God be a priority in your life?

Making God first should be your number one priority.

Making God your first priority is the best way of life. Matthew 6:33

Priority with God will give you direction.

You are God's priority and the apple of His eye.

If you have a church home, is it your priority?

Have you been so busy that you have not spent any time with the Lord?

If so, maybe it's time get your priorities straight-stop and pray.

Thought 37

RESPONSIBILITY

Again, it will be like a man going on a journey, who called his servants and entrusted his wealth to them. To one he gave five bags of gold, to another two bags, and to another one bag, each according to his ability. Then he went on his journey. The man who had received five bags of gold went at once and put his money to work and gained five bags more. So also, the one with two bags of gold gained two more. But the man who had received one bag went off, dug a hole in the ground and hid his master's money. **Matthew 25:14-18**

In your journey through life, are you giving God all He desires?

As a Christian, you have a responsibility in how you serve God.

If you proclaim to be a Christian, God should not have to wait for you to serve Him.

Once you have accepted Christ as your Lord and Savior, it's time to act!

Joining church is a responsibility.

As a Christian, others will be looking at you. It is your responsibility to live a Christ-like life.

Do you have a responsibility in your church home?

With responsibility comes accountability.

Are you a responsible Christian?

Being responsible requires work on your part.
Many people hesitate to join church because they do not want to be responsible. Are you one of them?

When it comes to Christ, are you willing to be responsible to him?

Christ was born on earth for one responsibility.....US!

Being responsible is not easy, and it becomes harder when we accept Christ.

Who are you responsible to? God made a personal investment in you. Was it worth it?

What are you doing with God's word? Is it in you?

One must be willing to act on the word of God, not just sit on it. Is God's investment growing in you?

Thought 38

SIN

Come now, let us settle the matter, says the LORD. Though your sins are like scarlet, they shall be as white as snow; though they are red as crimson, they shall be like wool. **Isaiah 1:18**

The Bible says that whoever knows the right thing to do and fails to do it, they have sinned.

God will forgive you for your sin, if you ask Him.

Have you committed a sin?

Many of you have sinned.

It is not good to sin against God.

Never use God's name in vain.

Many of us were lost and now we are found. Thank God.

It's not good to be in the presence of a jealous God.

If you know God, then why sin?

When you think about sinning and you think you're alone, remember God is there with you.

Sinning will come back to you, for you reap what you sow.

Sin is never a good thing.

All sin will soon come into the light.

You cannot hide your sin forever.

Two wrongs do not make a right

Man came into this world a sinner but it doesn't mean that you have to leave the same way.

Sin can make you mean.

Sin can separate you from God.

Sin is always looking for a way into your life. Don't let it in!

Many bad habits of this world are sinful.

Don't let sin into your life.

Staying close to God will help you fight sin.

Thought 39

TATTOOS

Do you not know that your bodies are temples of the Holy Spirit, who is in you, whom you have received from God? You are not your own; [20] you were bought at a price. Therefore honor God with your bodies.
1 Corinthians 6: 10-20

Are you treating your body at the level that Christ paid for it?

Some say tattoos are a sin before God. What do you think?

Some say tattooing is under the old law. What do you think?

Some say it doesn't matter what you do to your body; it's what God says.

What does God say about tattoos?

Do tattoos lift up God or the world?

A tattoo is a sin before God or is it?

Tattoos can inspire others to come to Christ.

What dwells in your temple, sin or goodness?

Tattoos are a personal inner expression of one's feelings on life.

Tattoos can be and are a symbol of freedom.

The world sometimes fears individuals who have tattoos.

Have you presented your body to Christ?

Does a tattoo make a person a bad person?

Is a tattoo a symbol of an occult?

Do you really know anything about tattoos?

Tattoos have a real meaning in life. Others need to take time to find out what the meaning is.

Don't be too quick to judge someone who has a tattoo. They could be your brother in Christ.

Do you believe that Christ paid the highest price for you when He died on the cross for your sin? If so, were you worth it?

Are you putting God's word in your temple?

Thought 40

THOUGHTS

Some say that the heart is the voice of man.

Have you ever thought about what your treasure is? Some believe that it is God, but their actions reflect otherwise.

Are you willing to trust God, even if you don't understand or can't see what He is doing?

I have one simple question to ask. When it comes to God, is your heart black or white?

Do you really have the spirit of God in you or is it just talk?

Do you really think about God or do you just talk about God?

If your life is upside down and your world is spinning, where is God when all this is happening?

Have you ever been so stubborn that no one could tell you anything?

Have you been so upset that your blood pressure is up?

People keep telling you that you don't listen, and all the while you're feeling sick and your world is a mess? I wonder why?

If your life is upside down, maybe it is time to try something new. Maybe God is using this message to plant a seed.

Are you ready for one of the secrets of life? "Try listening for once, you just might hear God."

How many of you are saying that it is always some else's fault (pointing the finger at others)? The Bible says to let a man examine himself; are you doing this?

Are you perfect? The answer is probably no.

When was the last time you looked in the mirror? Maybe the person in the mirror looking at you is the biggest problem in your life.

Maybe it is time to point your finger at yourself and try getting it right.

When you do get it right, then maybe you will have the right to complain.

Many of us read the word. We pray and then we say we love the Lord. Well, guess what? Do your actions reflect the Lord?

Where is your desire to work for the Lord?

Where is your desire to be committed to His kingdom?

Are you willing to trust God, even if you don't understand or can't see what He is doing?

Thought 41

WIVES

He who finds a wife finds a good thing and obtains favor from the Lord. **Proverbs 18:22**

A godly wife loves her godly husband unconditionally.

A wife is someone who loves you like God does.

A wife is to be treasured.

Most men need to listen to their wives more often; It may keep them out of trouble.

The Bible says a man who finds a good wife, finds a good thing.

If you want favor from the Lord, find a good wife.

Finding a wife can be a dream come true.

Having a good wife makes a husband feel good about coming home.

There's nothing like receiving a smile from your wife.

There is no love on earth better than the love from your wife.

True love can exist between a man and a woman.

A wife is someone special that a husband should take care of.

Is your wife like the virtuous woman in the Bible? See Proverbs 31.

A godly woman is truly a blessing from God.

Another attribute that a woman has is following her love for her God.

The love from your wife comes from God.

When looking for a wife, look within.

A godly wife is good to have when you are sick.

A godly wife will be a good mother.

God will honor a husband who respects his wife.

No godly husband or man should abuse his wife or woman.

Have you ever thanked God for your wife?

ABOUT THE AUTHOR

Pastor Vern H. Haynes, Jr. and his wife Sandra H. Haynes of twenty-two years settled in the city of Paso Robles, California. He is the father of five children. He retired from the California Youth Authority (State of California), after twenty- nine years of service. He was a Superintendent and the State Religious Coordinator for the department.

Educational Background:

1. Master of Arts in Counseling Psychology from National University, Stockton, CA.

2. Bachelor of Arts in Behavioral Science from National University, Stockton, CA.

3. Associate Degree of Arts from Cuesta College, San Luis Obispo, CA.

4. Ordained in 1996 under: "The Family Praise and Worship Ministries, Galt, CA; True Spirit Missionary Baptist Church, Paso Robles, CA; and Gloryland Baptist Church, Stockton, CA.

- (1997 -2013) Pastor Vern H. Haynes, Jr. and his wife Sandra H. Haynes were the founders of "Married For Life" a marriage counseling ministry. The vision of a marriage ministry was given to Pastor Haynes in 1997.

God wants marriages to be successful and to reflect the love that God has for his church. Married for Life is Bible based and its teaching is shared through counseling sessions, lectures, preaching, seminars, and individual meetings, small and large groups.

The focal points of "Married For Life" are to provide individuals, singles, and couples with the biblical knowledge and understanding of God's blueprint for marriage and to assist them in maintaining their marriage.

Husbands and wives must learn the concepts of what it takes to be that Godly man and woman and to treat each other with Godly love. It is the mission of "Married For Life" to bring God's people closer together and to have long, happy, and loving marriages in the name of Jesus.

- (1996 – 2002) Assistant Pastor and Youth Pastor at Family Praise and Worship, in Stockton, California. Active in men's groups and Promise Keepers.

- (2002 – 2006) Park Ministries-Conducted services in the Stockton City Park during 911 for approximately four months. Many souls were saved and were placed in churches in the surrounding community. During the same time, Pastor Haynes was the Church Administrator, Armor Bearer and Adviser to the Board of Directors and Pastor at Lifeseed Christian Fellowship Church in Stockton, CA.

- (2004 – 2009) Served as the Assistant & Youth Pastor at True Spirit Missionary Baptist Church in Atascadero, California. His many duties included but were not limited to: acting on behalf of the Pastor during his absences, Business office, Church business administrator, leading bible studies, men's groups, youth groups, Vacation Bible School, food bank, outreach programs and overseeing many other church activities.

- (2009 – 2010) Pastor Haynes was involved in evangelist work. During this time, pastoral care to pastors which provided them an outlet to talk freely regarding their ministries and other concerns.

- (2009 – Present) Senior Pastor of Family Praise & Worship.

Family Praise & Worship was founded in 2009 by Pastor Vern H. Haynes, Jr. and his wife Sandra H. Haynes. Family Praise & Worship is located in Templeton, California.

Family Praise and Worship is called to exalt the name of Jesus and uplift God's Kingdom by believing the Bible as the inspired Word of God and the sole authority for faith and practice while also declaring its purpose as follows:

To maintain regular services for public worship. To proclaim earnestly the Gospel message and to urge its personal acceptance, both privately and publicly. To promote systematic Bible study and teaching for Christian service and soul winning. To pray for one another that we may ever live according to the will of God, as revealed in His Word. To promote Christian fellowship and friendship. To promote the Christian education of our youth by training them in all things according to the precepts of the Word of God.

IT'S JUST A THOUGHT…